ALTERNATOR
BOOKS™

BLACK LIVES MATTER
From Hashtag to the Streets

Dr. Artika R. Tyner

Lerner Publications ◆ Minneapolis

Lerner Publications Company
An imprint of Lerner Publishing Group, Inc.
241 First Avenue North
Minneapolis, MN 55401 USA

For reading levels and more information, look up this title at www.lernerbooks.com.

Library of Congress Cataloging-in-Publication Data

Names: Tyner, Artika R., author.
Title: Black Lives Matter : from hashtag to the streets / Dr. Artika R. Tyner.
Description: Minneapolis : Lerner Publications , 2021. | Series: The fight for Black rights | Includes webography. | Includes bibliographical references and index. | Audience: Ages 8–12 years | Audience: Grades 4–6 | Summary: "Started as a hashtag after the death of Trayvon Martin, Black Lives Matter has become one of the most significant protest movements of our time. See how its activists and demonstrators have changed the course of history"— Provided by publisher.
Identifiers: LCCN 2020039176 (print) | LCCN 2020039177 (ebook) | ISBN 9781728429564 (Library Binding) | ISBN 9781728430232 (Paperback) | ISBN 9781728429625 (eBook)
Subjects: LCSH: Black lives matter movement—Juvenile literature. | African Americans—Civil rights—Juvenile literature. | United States—Race relations—Juvenile literature. | Racial profiling in law enforcement—United States—Juvenile literature. | African Americans—Social conditions—21st century—Juvenile literature. | African Americans—Violence against—Juvenile literature. | Police brutality—United States—Juvenile literature. | Political participation—United States—History—Juvenile literature. | Civil rights movements—United States—History—21st century—Juvenile literature. | Political activists—United States—History—Juvenile literature. | Kaepernick, Colin, 1987—-Juvenile literature. | Garza, Alicia, 1981—-Juvenile literature. | Racism—United States—History—21st century—Juvenile literature.
Classification: LCC E185.615 .T95 2021 (print) | LCC E185.615 (ebook) | DDC 323.1196/073—dc23

LC record available at https://lccn.loc.gov/2020039176
LC ebook record available at https://lccn.loc.gov/2020039177

Manufactured in the United States of America
1 – CG – 12/31/20

Table of Contents

CHAPTER 1

SILENT
Protest

On September 1, 2016, all eyes were on 49ers quarterback Colin Kaepernick. At the game a week earlier, he had sat on the bench during the US national anthem. This time, he knelt on the sideline. Kaepernick continued to kneel throughout the season. He was protesting police brutality against Black people.

Kaepernick was one of the most promising quarterbacks in the National Football League (NFL). Some supported his right to protest, but he received strong criticism from NFL fans and owners. Kaepernick was released at the end of the 2016 season. He was no longer in the NFL. But he continued to advocate against police brutality.

Kaepernick's protest brought new attention to the issue of racial injustice in America. For that moment, he became the face of the Black Lives Matter movement.

During the first week of the 2016 NFL season, eleven players knelt during the national anthem with Kaepernick. One of them was Eric Reid (*left*) of the San Francisco 49ers.

THE BIRTH OF A MOVEMENT

In 2012, a seventeen-year-old Black boy named Trayvon Martin was killed while walking home. Alicia Garza was tired of seeing the senseless killings of Black people. She was frustrated that Trayvon's killer was not found guilty. She first used the phrase "Black lives matter" in a 2013 Facebook post. Her friend, Patrisse Cullors, added a hashtag. #BlackLivesMatter went viral.

In April 2012, protesters marched silently through Los Angeles, California. They were demanding justice for Trayvon Martin.

Black Lives Matter cofounder Alicia Garza spoke at the 2018 Women's March in Las Vegas, Nevada.

The Civil Rights Movement of the 1950s and 1960s ended decades ago. Yet Black people still face police violence. Many experience unfair legal treatment. Garza, Cullors, and Opal Tometi founded Black Lives Matter to fight for change. Its members call for respect and the protection of rights for Black people. They demand fair laws to protect Black people. People of all ages and backgrounds have joined their efforts. There are now Black Lives Matter groups across the globe.

RISING UP

Black Lives Matter became a battle cry for justice. It shined a light on the injustices Black people experience.

For the next seven years, Black Lives Matter supporters protested the deaths of Black people. Some, like Trayvon, were killed by people in their community. Many of them had been killed by the police. Eric Garner, Michael Brown, Tamir Rice, Freddie Gray, Alton Sterling, Philando Castile, Isaiah Lewis, and Breonna Taylor are just some of the victims of police violence since 2014. Their killers thought they looked suspicious or appeared to be a threat.

Eric Garner was killed by police on July 17, 2014. Five years later on July 17, 2019, people gathered in Staten Island, New York, to demand justice for his death.

Laquan McDonald was seventeen when he was killed by Chicago police in 2014. When a video was released in 2015 showing that Laquan was walking away when he was shot and killed, protesters took to the streets to demand justice for his death.

Black Lives Matter supporters held peaceful protests across the US. They were often met with force. Police officers threw tear gas into crowds. They shot rubber bullets at protesters. The First Amendment protects the right to protest. However, some protesters are arrested for violating curfew or blocking traffic.

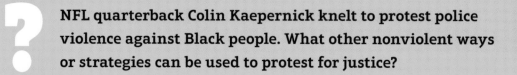

? NFL quarterback Colin Kaepernick knelt to protest police violence against Black people. What other nonviolent ways or strategies can be used to protest for justice?

CHAPTER 2

A LONG
History

Violence and oppression have been part of the Black experience in the United States since before it was a country. Black people first arrived on slave ships in 1619. They were treated like property instead of humans. They were not given the same rights as white people.

After the Civil War (1861–1865), enslaved Americans were freed and given citizenship. The Thirteenth and Fourteenth Amendments were meant to protect the rights of Black people. The Thirteenth Amendment ended slavery, and the Fourteenth Amendment promised equal rights for everyone. But states created Black Codes and Jim Crow laws. These laws were meant to limit the freedoms of Black Americans. The laws also kept Black people separate from white people in a practice called segregation. In 1896, the US Supreme Court ruled that segregation was legal.

During segregation, Black people and white people were kept separate. There were many rules, including not being able to use the same bathrooms, drink from the same water fountains, or swim in the same pools.

ORGANIZED PROTESTS

During the Civil Rights Movement, Black people organized nonviolent protests to fight for their rights. The Montgomery Bus Boycott was the first major demonstration of the movement.

In 1955, fifteen-year-old Claudette Colvin was arrested in Montgomery, Alabama. She had refused to give up her seat on a public bus to a white passenger. Nine months later, Rosa Parks was arrested for doing the same. The Black community refused to ride public buses. They wanted the bus system to be desegregated. The boycott lasted 381 days. The bus system was desegregated on December 21, 1956.

On December 21, 1956, Dr. Martin Luther King Jr. and other civil rights leaders celebrated the desegregation of the bus system by sitting in the front of a Montgomery city bus.

The successful boycott showed that organized protests worked. Civil rights activists planned more protests to end segregation in all public spaces. Students organized more bus protests. Others led sit-ins at lunch counters. Malcolm X and Martin Luther King Jr. emerged as leaders of the movement during this time. The protests were national news and made Black civil rights a key political issue.

Ida B. Wells

JULY 16, 1862–MARCH 25, 1931

Ida B. Wells was a journalist, suffragist, and civil rights advocate. She called for the rights of all Americans to be protected. Wells wrote and spoke about the history of Black lynchings. She was one of the founders of the National Association for the Advancement of Colored People (NAACP).

DEATH AND DESTRUCTION

The fight for equality was not easy. Many white people did not want segregation to end. Civil rights protesters were regularly met with violence. Peaceful protesters were threatened and beaten. Homes and churches were burned. Some, including Malcolm X and Martin Luther King Jr., were killed.

The 1963 March on Washington was a gathering of more than 250,000 people in front of the Lincoln Memorial in Washington, DC. The protesters were demanding equal rights for all Americans.

Dr. Martin Luther King Jr. *(center)* led the march from Selma to Montgomery with his wife, Coretta Scott King, and other civil rights leaders.

One of the largest demonstrations of violence during the Civil Rights Movement happened on March 7, 1965. Protesters marched from Selma, Alabama, to Montgomery. During the march, state troopers attacked the marchers. Fifty-eight people were injured. The day became known as Bloody Sunday.

Despite serious violence against them, Black people kept marching. They continued protesting and fighting for freedom.

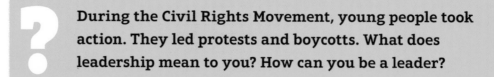

? During the Civil Rights Movement, young people took action. They led protests and boycotts. What does leadership mean to you? How can you be a leader?

CHAPTER 3

CONTINUING THE
Fight

In May of 2020, police responded to a call from a Minneapolis store. Four officers arrested George Floyd for using what the clerk thought was a fake twenty-dollar bill. Witnesses said Floyd was not resisting arrest. A white officer held his knee on Floyd's neck. Floyd repeatedly said that he could not breathe. The officer held his knee there for over eight minutes until Floyd stopped moving. He was later pronounced dead.

Floyd's death reignited support for Black Lives Matter. Hundreds of protests were held in the US. People took to the streets on nearly every continent. Protesters came from all races, ages, and backgrounds. The global outcry and protests led to the quick arrests of the officers who killed Floyd.

Hundreds of people visited the George Floyd memorial in Minneapolis, Minnesota. They left flowers, gifts, and art.

Protesters and organizers use phones to record inspiring moments, spread stories of injustice, and tell people where and when to meet for rallies and marches.

#SAYTHEIRNAMES

Social media has become a tool for organizing protests. It reaches all ages, especially teenagers and people in their twenties. Grouping tools such as hashtags can connect people who share a common passion across the globe. When many people use a hashtag, is it more likely to appear in social media feeds, where more people will see it. #BlackLivesMatter had been shared on Twitter nearly 50 million times by September 2020.

Another hashtag popular within the Black Lives Matter movement is #SayTheirNames. The hashtag is used to honor the individual victims of police violence. It was inspired by #SayHerName, a hashtag created to highlight the fact that public attention often focuses on Black men who have been killed and not Black women.

The hashtag #ShareTheMicNow was created to elevate the voices of Black women. On Instagram, Black women took over the accounts of white women influencers. The action was symbolic of creating space for underrepresented voices.

Me Too Movement

Tarana Burke organized the Me Too movement. She built a global community to end sexual harassment and assault. Thousands of people were brought together under the #MeToo hashtag to protect the rights of women against physical and sexual violence.

PAINTING THE LANDSCAPE

Throughout history, Black artists have used their skills to fight for racial justice. Artists continue to use their pens and paintbrushes to stand for justice and freedom. Black Lives Matter art and literature are tools for organizing movements. It brings people together to share their stories and change policies. Street art supporting Black people and Black Lives Matter can be seen across the country.

Black Lives Matter murals were painted on city streets across the United States during the summer of 2020. In New York City, a mural was painted in front of Trump Tower.

On July 5, 2020, in Annapolis, Maryland, artists painted a mural of Breonna Taylor. She was killed by police on March 13, 2020.

BLACK LIVES MATTER

BREONNA TAYLOR
June 5, 1993–
March 13, 2020

Additionally, there have been calls for white celebrities and entertainment leaders to step down from their roles. Alexis Ohanian, cofounder of Reddit, left his job at the company. He asked for a Black person to fill his seat. The goal is to provide space for Black leaders and to create equal access and opportunities.

 Hashtags connect people so they can work on issues together. In what other ways can social media be used to educate and organize people?

CHAPTER 4

WHAT COMES **Next?**

Black Lives Matter protesters have demanded changes in how police work. Some have called for defunding the police. Defunding would mean that communities spend less money on policing and put money into other community programs. The ultimate goal is to protect Black lives and create safe neighborhoods.

Some cities started changing their policies within weeks of Floyd's death. In New York City, money was taken from the police budget and given to social and youth services instead. Members of the Minneapolis city council pledged to disband the city's police department. They plan to create a new model for public safety.

Protesters are not just voicing outrage. They want change. In late June 2020, protesters camped out for two nights in front of New York City Hall demanding a $1.3 billion cut from the police budget. They want that money to go to other services that support the community.

BLACK
LIVES
MATTER

ORK CITY WORKERS
OR JUSTICE
ICE REFORM NOW · BLACK L

CHANGING THE LAW

Following the protests, laws banning choke holds were passed in many states, from Arizona to Connecticut. A choke hold is used to restrain someone by cutting off or restricting their breathing. The laws are meant to protect Black people from police violence. Some police departments are making the change before state laws are passed. In June 2020, the Dallas police department banned any force that would block a person's airway.

Both George Floyd and Eric Garner repeatedly said "I can't breathe" before being killed by police. The phrase has been used while protesting police violence since 2014.

Representative Karen Bass from California is one of the writers of the George Floyd Justice in Policing Act. On June 25, 2020, she spoke in front of the Capitol Building in Washington, DC, to encourage nationwide police reform.

Officers are being trained in problem-solving and communication. Many hope that officers will use these skills to de-escalate situations that could otherwise turn violent. Police departments are also speeding up the release of body camera videos. The videos show how officers interact with the public. They are intended to provide evidence in cases of police brutality.

In 2020, Congress proposed the George Floyd Justice in Policing Act. The law would ban choke holds and no-knock warrants across the country. It calls for changes in police training and would require all officers to wear body cameras.

CHANGING ATTITUDES

Since Colin Kaepernick left the NFL, support for the Black Lives Matter movement has grown. It is now a statement used by people around the country and the world who seek racial justice. Entire sports teams are kneeling in support of Black Lives Matter. The NFL and US soccer have lifted their bans on kneeling during the anthem.

The Kaepernick Foundation launched a legal defense fund for protesters in 2020. Other pro athletes and celebrities have taken a vocal stand against police brutality. They are donating funds to support protesters who need legal help.

The Black Lives Matter movement has inspired thousands of people to stand up for racial justice in big and small ways. Its supporters have shown that change is possible when they stand together.

Unity for Racial Justice

The 2020 Excellence in Sports Performance Yearly (ESPY) Award ceremony honored the Black Lives Matter movement. The hosts, Sue Bird, Megan Rapinoe, and Russell Wilson, spoke about ending systemic racism. Bird called for the dignity of Black people to be respected at all times, not just when they are playing sports. Rapinoe encouraged white people to act as allies in the fight for Black rights. Wilson shared his dream for his children to see the end of hundreds of years of oppression in the United States.

Both the Oklahoma City Thunder and the Houston Rockets took a knee during the national anthem before Game Two of the 2020 Western Conference NBA Playoffs.

? Kaepernick stood up for what he believed in even when it wasn't popular. Have you ever stood up for an idea or for a friend that wasn't popular?

BLACK LIVES MATTER
Timeline

May 17, 1954: The US Supreme Court rules segregation in public schools unconstitutional.

March 2, 1955: Fifteen-year-old Claudette Colvin is arrested. Nine months later, Rosa Parks is also arrested.

December 5, 1955: The Montgomery Bus Boycott begins. Thousands of people refuse to ride the bus for 381 days.

February 21, 1965: Civil rights activist Malcolm X is shot and killed while giving a speech in New York City.

April 4, 1968: Civil rights leader Rev. Dr. Martin Luther King Jr. is shot and killed in Memphis, Tennessee.

February 26, 2012: Seventeen-year-old Trayvon Martin is killed.

July 13, 2013: Trayvon Martin's killer is found not guilty. The hashtag #BlackLivesMatter is used for the first time.

September 1, 2016: Colin Kaepernick kneels at a preseason 49ers game.

May 25, 2020: George Floyd is killed by a police officer in Minneapolis, Minnesota.

June 8, 2020: Congress introduces the George Floyd Justice in Policing Act.

Glossary

advocate: to speak out about a cause

body camera: a device worn by the police to record police interactions with community members

choke hold: the use of force to block a person's airway, restricting their breathing

city council: a group of elected officials who oversee city laws and policies

de-escalate: to lower the risk of violence

dignity: the state of being worthy of respect and honor

lynching: a killing, most often by hanging, of a person by a group without due process

no-knock warrant: a document that allows police to enter a person's home without knocking or ringing the doorbell

suffragist: a person advocating for voting rights

Supreme Court: the highest court in the United States

systemic racism: patterns and policies that enforce discrimination based upon race

Learn More

Black Lives Matter: Britannica for Kids
https://kids.britannica.com/kids/article/Black-Lives-Matter/632612

Black Lives Matter: Teaching Kids News
https://teachingkidsnews.com/2020/06/09/black-lives-matter/

The Civil Rights Movement: Scholastic News
https://sn4.scholastic.com/pages/text-sets/the-civil-rights-movement.html

Harris, Duchess. *Black Lives Matter*. Minneapolis: Core Library, 2018.

Hoena, Blake. *Colin Kaepernick: Athletes Who Made a Difference*. Minneapolis: Graphic Universe, 2020.

Tyner, Dr. Artika R. *Vigilante Danger: A Threat to Black Lives*. Minneapolis: Lerner Publications, 2021.

Index

Photo Acknowledgments

The images in this book are used with the permission of: Thearon W. Henderson/Getty Images, p. 5; David McNew/Getty Images, p. 6; Sam Morris/Getty Images, p. 7; Spencer Platt/Getty Images, p. 8; Scott Olson/Getty Images, p. 9; Russell Lee/Library of Congress/Wikimedia, p. 11; Everett Collection/Newscom, p. 12; Sallie Garrity/National Portrait Gallery/Wikimedia, p. 13; DALMAS/SIPA/Newscom, p. 14; Ivan Massar/Black Star/Newscom, p. 15; Brandon Bell/Getty Images, p. 17; Win McNamee/Getty Images, p. 18; Kris Connor/Comedy Centra/Getty Images, p. 19; David Dee Delgado/Getty Images, p. 20; Patrick Smith/Getty Images, p. 21; Stephanie Keith/Getty Images, p. 23; Stephen Maturen/Getty Images, p. 24; Alex Wong/Getty Images, p. 25; Kevin C. Cox/Getty Images, p. 27; rosiekeystrokes/Pixabay, background

Cover: Ezra Shaw/Getty Images, left; Stephanie Keith/Getty Images, middle; Samuel Corum/Getty Images, right